TO KN□ □□□□

JENNIFER JACKSON BERRY

TO KNOW CRUSH © 2020 BY JENNIFER JACKSON BERRY
THIS IS AN EARLY EDITION ONLY AVAILABLE DIRECTLY
FROM THE PUBLISHER AND THE AUTHOR.

COVER ART: *FAT EMBRACE*, © SAM RAWLS, 2019
COVER & INTERIOR DESIGN: ALBAN FISCHER

ISBN 978-1-936919-79-6
PRINTED IN THE UNITED STATES OF AMERICA
LIBRARY OF CONGRESS CATALOGING-IN-PUBLICATION
DATA IS AVAILABLE UPON REQUEST.

PUBLISHED BY YESYES BOOKS
1614 NE ALBERTA ST
PORTLAND, OR 97211
YESYESBOOKS.COM

KMA SULLIVAN, PUBLISHER
STEVIE EDWARDS, SENIOR EDITOR, BOOK DEVELOPMENT
ALBAN FISCHER, GRAPHIC DESIGNER
COLE HILDEBRAND, SENIOR EDITOR OF OPERATIONS
LUTHER HUGHES, ASSISTANT EDITOR & YYB TWITTER
AMBER RAMBHAROSE, EDITOR, ART LIFE & INSTAGRAM
ALEXIS SMITHERS, ASSISTANT EDITOR, VINYL & YYB FACEBOOK
PHILLIP B. WILLIAMS, COEDITOR IN CHIEF, *VINYL*
AMIE ZIMMERMAN, EVENTS COORDINATOR

*for Mike*

*because we know crush*

*Being fat and happy and in love is a radical act.*

—LINDY WEST

*Nope*, I wanted to say to the old man at the diner
on a Sunday morning when he asked if there was
any food left inside, *ate every egg, poached, fried,*
*& scrambled. I'm wearing syrup like perfume—*
*here, come closer, smell me. I'll meet you halfway*
*across the parking lot.*

*Oops, that's a hash brown burp.*

*You should have seen me: I palmed pancakes*
*& rolled sausage links from cheek to cheek.*

*They might be serving lunch soon, you should go in*
*& check. No grilled cheese though—I used the last*
*of the butter pats to help me slip from the booth.*

*My husband watched.*

there was a kiss electric & a time you moved your
hands from where they held my knees apart down my
inner thighs i screamed & came or came & screamed
it is a blur i can only describe with the word *fuck*
the *u* drawn out like a furling & unfurling snake

I once paid for a month of Beautiful Agony.

User-uploaded videos, masturbator's face only.

The only porn I've ever paid for. Fade to black
seconds after orgasm.

We are all fat in different ways.

I would be bored now.

Every time I write about sex it is a radical act because someone thought it was ok to sell lingerie one-size-fits-all.

I told the waiter at another diner we'd pay for the
sad man's meal. He was missing his dead wife.
He was loud & sloppy-crying.

Another couple had already paid for him.
The waiter brought us two chocolate chip cookies
instead of his check.

That will be one of us, one at a two-top, blowing
snot into a napkin.

Some statistics say it will be me.

Some statistics say it will be you.

We ate the cookies anyway.

sometimes when our curves fit seamless you whisper
*i could sleep like this* meaning you're satisfied meaning
you're mine meaning you could die like this meaning
die like this & be happy meaning i could die like this
meaning nightly against your body meaning our
bellies are the softest pillows in the house

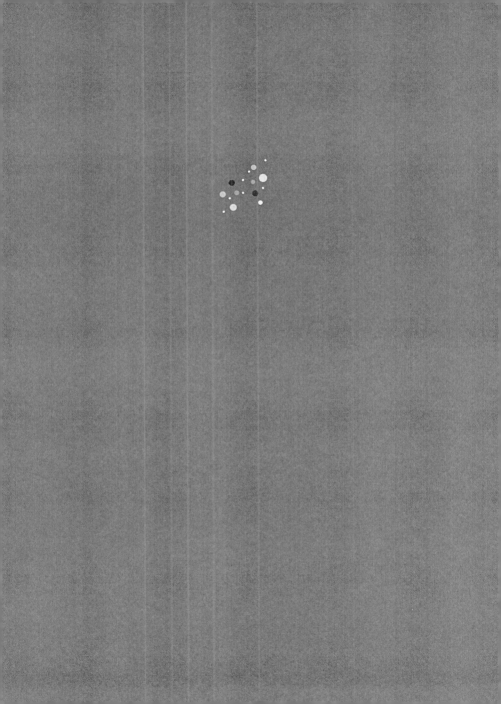

I have no origin story, no double-chinned phoenix
doubling her size rising from ashes of trauma.

No fiery ghost-fingers to expel from memory,
no fiery fingers to repel in the future.

I haven't created layer upon layer to protect.

Nothing happened so deep I had to eat to keep
the world from seeing me.

There is no bowl of mother's milk too empty
or too full. True I inherited a sweet tooth
but there was no binge purge cycle spun.

I am not a cautionary tale.
I am not a before picture.

Sometimes to fall asleep I think of the farm
where we were married, the moment I saw you
through a row of trees as we circled from different
sides of the lodge toward the arbor at the edge
of the pond.

I end the day thinking of the rooster that crowed
during the mid-afternoon ceremony.

When I go down on you, there is so much to bury
my face—you smell like the beginning.

Sometimes your belly pushes on my clit
when we fuck. That is a different beginning.

One that ends a moment later.
One to recapture any time we want.

A Plump Wife & A Big Barn Never Did Any Man
Harm. Antique store find: this aphorism on a trivet.

I buy it for irony. I could hurt you with a thunder
thigh squeeze, a motorboat suffocation.

I'm debating whether to hang this as a makeshift
plaque or place every hot pot on it.

I joke *when I sit around the barn, I sit* around
*the barn.* When the barn door opens, so plump.

There is harm done sometimes taking the pressure
off, like once the body knows crush
the organs are rearranged.

Like every time I ask you say—*no, you're not
hurting me.*

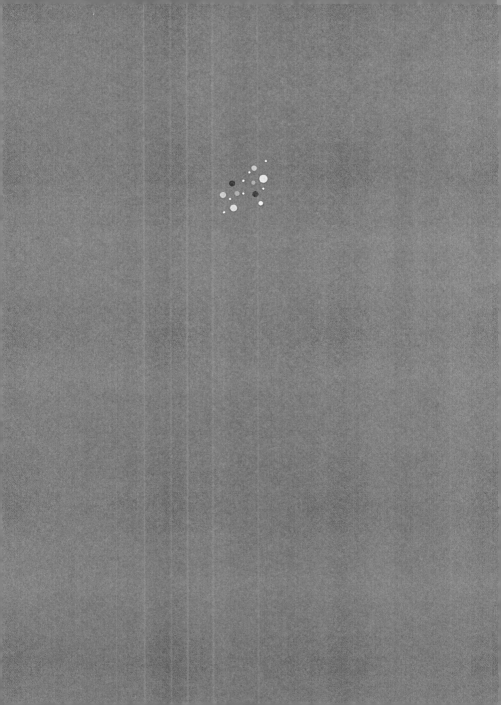

Brave is wearing a tank top?
Brave is wearing a crop top?

Been called brave in print, in book reviews,
on podcast interviews.

*Brave* is getting on top.

Only been called healthy once—at a house party.
By a man trying to sleep with me.

When I hear paper crinkle under my ass, I know
I'm about to be scolded.

The hair at the back of my neck bristles.

I'm a dog ready to fight.

My first doctor had a gin nose.

My second doctor told me it happened to all fat kids
when I asked why my face got so red at recess.

I was six.

Every time I write about sex it is a radical act because
I didn't go to the gynecologist for the first time
until I was 33.

I got my first cold sore at forty.

I didn't know what it was so I picked at it like I would
a pimple.

Doctors think it could happen like this every time:
I just point at my fat & they know the reason for my
visit. But this time that's what I did.

Pointed at that fucker bloomed on my chin.

Forty. My body continues to surprise.

& each other's bodies, the ones we think we know
are changing.

That patch of skin near your left armpit where
my hand lands when you're on your back, my head
in the crook of your neck. It used to make you
shudder when I'd circle my fingertips there.

Remember those few months when your finger
grew wild with nerve endings? It was the strangest
thing. I could make you hard just fingertip to
fingertip.

You named skin between my breasts plushy. Softer
than anywhere else. It has since roughened to match
the rest of my body.

Teenagers playing True Colors posing questions
to the group, each to answer with the name of
someone at the table.

I slapped the card back down question unplayed,
pushing it under the others, hiding:

*Who would you recognize in the dark?*

I was afraid I'd win the round, my name
on everyone's lips.

Even though two of them had dated for years.

Even though no one had touched me yet.

Every time I write about sex it is a radical act because
Fat Monica had to tell Chandler he was caressing
couch cushions in the dark.

I used too many calendars marking each Monday
the day life would begin.

I stepped on too many scales thinking that could be
a first step to anything new.

I spent too many years a player piano making music
without being touched.

*Never have I ever gone down on a Dannon Yogurt truck driver.* It's how friends got me every time. I was the only one to drink.

His handle on message boards was Footlong.

He wasn't.

He asked me to take off my shirt.

I didn't.

Another drunk circle I admitted my numbers. Blow jobs far exceeding instances of intercourse.

Someone said he liked the odds of getting in my mouth.

Every time I write about sex it is a radical act because
there is another game: Would You Rather? As in
would you rather date a woman with a history
of STIs or a woman 100 lbs. overweight?

what if i hadn't waited for you to be the first one
to touch my stomach the first one to tell me my
shoulders are sexy what if i hadn't waited for you to
be the first one to see me naked standing up what if i
hadn't waited for you what if i hadn't waited for you
what if I hadn't waited for you

But what if I had thought of it as a choice to wait?

But what if I thought *I* was worth waiting for?

But what if I had wanted to be seen while I was waiting?

foreplay now is my eyes on varicose ropes twisted under your skin is my finger along the vein riffling your upper thigh is stretching your toes back is loosening tendons is your palm against hot bruises is your eyes on my injection sites is making my sludge blood rush

A co-worker says he doesn't bother hitting the cat
when it's bad because *she's too fat to feel it.*

I remember walking high school halls, upper-class
boys would push each other into me. More than
twenty years I'm still trying to figure out the theory
of the push. Embarrass him? Embarrass me?

It happened when I was alone.

It happened when I was with someone. I had to
pretend to be ok.

Was the pusher hoping I'd like it? Then want
his friend in every way I could want someone?

Then he'd be embarrassed by the love of a fat girl.

Another co-worker responds: *Hit the cat anyway.*

I saw a large woman sitting on a tipped-over Target
cart waiting for the bus the first warm day of
Spring, legs wide.

I think of the news story: *Target Apologizes for
Labeling Plus Size Dress Manatee Gray*.

Brave is a makeshift seat?
Brave is a lawn chair, an airplane seat?

The cart was cock red & thick plastic, buckling.

*Brave* is taking up space.

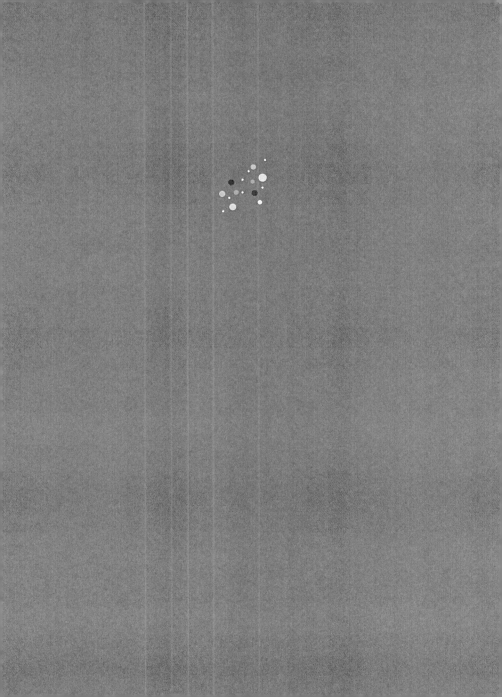

We've never flown anywhere together.

We took to the road from early on—first trip
to the closest White Castle in Zanesville, Ohio.
You'd only eaten the sliders from grocery
store freezers.

I put a chicken ring on my finger, snapped a pic.
Posted it with another artistic shot of crumpled
papers, thinned see-through with greasy sheen.

When we do plan that first flight, you'll tell me
about Delta's Comfort+ & I'll tell you
about Southwest's Customer of Size policy.

We'll both know we'll want to pre-board.

We'll put the arm rest up.

Our knees will touch.

Our sides will touch.

Our shoulders will touch.

Every time I write about sex it is a radical act because
I've yet to see a post about the mile-high club
in the Flying While Fat Facebook group, only
about absolute fear of seat spillage & being forced
off the plane.

I get that extra seat.

No one puts their carry-on on my extra seat.

I'm always going to be extra.

& I'm not going back to believing that's a problem.

I wouldn't trade the road trips though—from when
I didn't even think of flying. We slept in fifteen
different beds on our honeymoon to the Grand
Canyon.

The cool sheets in Vegas felt like a whisper after
the cacophony under the Freemont Street canopy,
asphalt heat creeping up our legs.

I don't remember John Wayne's bed at the Apache
Motel being all that comfortable, but I did sleep
through the alarm saying *I've seen enough rocks*.
We missed the Arches National Park & Moab
is only a memory of a trio of buffalo & elk & boar
skewers from dinner the night before.

There are some beds I only remember what we
woke for: slow dancing on the deck of the Belle
of Louisville, bourbon balls melting on our tongues.

In Sedona we had loud sex. The motel owner
wished she had realized a Pennsylvania couple was
coming.

She would have given a discount in exchange for
Sheetz coffee & a box of Tasty Kakes.

You put your hand over my mouth.

*Thin walls* you said.

I wanted everyone to know.

have you ever kissed someone pumping gas in an elevator in the cereal aisle i ask then sidle up & make the answer yes have you ever kissed someone waiting in line waiting for a manager for a test result for a rental car to be pulled around i make the answer yes have you ever kissed someone in the snow in her mittens because your gloves are wet from shoveling an hour ago yes in the middle of the street yes have you ever kissed someone on a do-not-walk answer yes on a do-not-stop on a don't-stop-don't-stop-don't-stop knowing yes the press of my yes of my body asking yes for a kiss

Third wheel on a mini-golf date with my best friend
when I was twelve, we saw two fat people
making out on a bench at the 18th hole.

Trinkets from every trip in a small plate on the TV
stand: Sun Studios guitar pick, mussel shell opened
but still hinged like a heart, a red rock, the tiniest
white Adirondack chair.

We laughed at them kissing, their fat hands moving
up & down each other.

It takes two quarters to make a flat penny.

It wasn't funny. Those bodies. Those hands. Those
were the first like mine I saw taking pleasure.

It takes two quarters to make a flat penny. We stand
& watch two steel rollers pressing.

When the dude who flips dough at Villa Reale said
*hi* to me on the bus, remembered me from the lunch
line waiting for my slice, I thought it might be time
for a change.

But I can't quit the place—I love the woman at the
cash register who dropped a plate of pasta as she
turned to deliver it to the counter & just sighed
& walked away, no clean-up, no apologetic nod to
the hungry customer, no yell back to the line cook
for another.

but the only time we turn our backs to each other is to change who is the outside spoon & who is the outside spoon is who reaches around & who reaches around finds what's hidden & what's hidden is hidden in folds of flesh & what's hidden in folds & what's hidden in flesh are secrets of how we love & how we love is hard & how we love is full & how we love cleans up messes & acknowledges the hunger & yells for more always & always yells for more

Every time I write about sex it is a radical act because
the myth of a sandwich falling from the folds
of a body is reinvented each time a really fat person
dies.

Every time I write about sex it is a radical act because
Melissa McCarthy fellates a sandwich in
*Bridesmaids*.

A group of men were harassing me & my sister
& our friend at Denny's. One turned the sandwich
name into a taunt: *Moons Over My Hammy!*

School yard lilt to his voice, emphasis on "my."

We knew our fat asses were the moons,
his dick the hammy.

But every time I write about sex it is a radical act because I've also heard the joke: *Fat chicks are like mopeds, fun to ride, but you don't want your friends to see you on one.*

The first doctor to examine Mama Cass Elliott after she died saw the ham sandwich & made it larger than her life.

He said she choked on it.

She died from a heart attack, weak heart arguably harmed further by crash dieting.

Every time I write about sex it is a radical act because fantasies were born for me in re-runs of cartoon Cass making love to all the kinds of candy while Scooby & Shaggy watched.

Her sandwich untouched.

you are cold pizza i crave you in the morning even
after last night i touch myself early hard breath quick
against my full pillow like the sloppy burp late when
i finish with you

My first mental health professional said his book would help. How to make yourself happy or some shit.

I was fourteen.

He said I didn't have to come back for follow-up. My parents bought the book. I didn't read it.

My second mental health professional didn't want to prescribe anything. Though the pills might help, I'd likely gain weight.

He said that would make me sadder.

My third mental health professional said *No,*
*some women get angry.*

I was in my early 20s & asked her *Aren't all women*
*embarrassed by street harassment?*

I was afraid someone would ask for directions on
campus to Goodbody Hall & I'd have to say *good* &
*body* in the same breath.

If there had been Snapchat I would have never left
the apartment.

Anger finally potholed the surface of my face I had
tried so hard to keep flat.

I remapped my fat-shaming brain.

Every time I write about sex it is a radical act because
some mornings there are still intrusive thoughts,
roundabouts circling but never giving exit.

A woman passed me a note after a reading: *I know your pain fuels your art, but have you tried Overeaters Anonymous?*

A woman flipped through my book at a signing: *I'm writing a book too. I have a formula. You can lose 100 lbs. in 14 months.*

She didn't mean some universal *you*. She meant me.

She looked me up & down.

She meant me.

Only been told I don't deserve this.

*This* is anything. Everything—good sex, any sex,
love, success, safety.

Been told only way to deserve anything is to change
my body. Cabbage Patch Kid promised to a child
for a five lb. loss. I can't count how many times
I joined Weight Watchers or how many times
my parents offered to pay the weekly fees.

I used to have a big tote of clothes in the back
of the closet, all too small, ready to be worn
on dates I'd have after I lost the weight.

I planned trips to the lake with friends several years
without getting in the water myself or even owning
a bathing suit.

Now my breasts like buoys lift in water.

Gently I tell myself I deserve this.

I'm weightless, thighs slide past each other easily
as I scissor.

I spin, I flip, I kick.

I let myself go.

I've let myself go.

I've let myself go to the water. I've let myself go
to anger to why did I wait so long then to peace.

I've let myself go to peace with my body.

I've let myself go.

I let it all go.

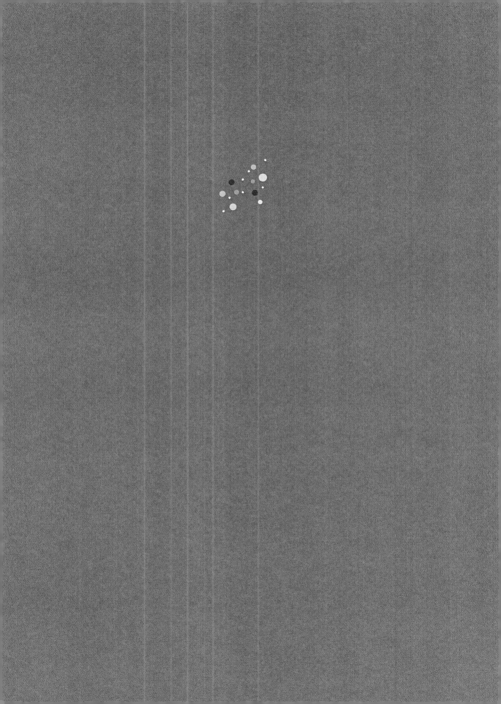

I remember one girl's OA story about her best
friend, how they sat on a tattered couch in front
of the TV popping M&Ms, an afternoon ritual
a 3 lb. bag each.

As of that meeting time, that Tuesday evening
in the cool autumn of a college town, she told us
she wasn't friends with her bad influence anymore.

My bad influence had gastric bypass right around
that same time.

We would skip our 3 o'clock class to eat our first
dinner, horribly orange Chinese food at the student
union food court.

I became her bad influence the night before her
wedding: Beef N Cheddars at the hotel bar from
the Arby's across the street. The cheese sauce
the same sick orange.

She looked beautiful the next day. Sleeveless &
glittered.

I binged on tequila & don't remember most of the
reception. I knocked on her brother's door back at
the hotel. I'm glad now he didn't answer, but wasn't
then.

The only reason I thought he *might* open the door
was because he was big & fat too.

Every time I write about sex it is a radical act because Ralph & Alice Kramden. Fred & Wilma, Homer & Marge, Peter & Lois. Kevin James & Leah Remini twice. Uncle Phil & Aunt Viv. Tony & Carmela Soprano. Turtle & all of his girlfriends, Sipowicz & all of his wives.

Sometimes I think of the skinny guy from the bar.
It always takes a few hours to remember
his name. I don't remember how we ended up
at his place. I remember there was a dog
& dog hair everywhere.

In the middle of it he stopped & asked
had I ever done this before. Neither of us could
seem to negotiate an angle around my belly or
my thighs that allowed for deep enough penetration.

Instead of admitting I had the same problem
the one other time, I just shook my head no.

He stood up & put on sweatpants.

He went to sleep.

I snuck out past the dog.

In the beginning I put my hands around his waist
& I swear it seemed like my forefingers & thumbs
touched. His hard abdomen was strange to me.

Now I wish I really had closed a circle of my two
hands at his navel.

& squeezed.

Until his head popped off. That I would have
remembered.

What Shallow Hal could have done with the purple
thong instead of just dismissing its size:

felt the fabric that had been so close
to his lover just moments before, thumb & pointer
finger in circles like the best way circles can be
in the bedroom, slow & soft & never-stopping,

or brought it to his face, inhaled slow & deep
& always-deeper,

or anything else really, anything but dismissal.

It is the central question of the movie: how does Hal
touch Rosemary without knowing she's fat?
Doesn't he feel the jiggle as she tenses,
notice the span of her back as she arches?

Doesn't he see his own hands cradling farther apart
than his brain says they should be?

Isn't it always someone's broken brain?

i would never want to not know it was your body
to not know your body to not know your skin's
dimpling & pull to not know your belly fat & soft &
stretch-marked i would never want to not know each
hair on your back or to ever know again stubble there
like after the one time we shaved it at your insistence
i would never want to not know your back's fuzz
against my cheek i would never want to not know
your body i would never want to not see your body
walking towards the bed

You see me.

You ask to put your hands under my breasts
when you're cold, knowing the heat that's there,
a satisfied sigh as you warm.

A tiny moan when your extended thumbs find my
nipples.

I wanted a Ta-Ta Towel until I saw the price, $45.

I *am* fed up with boob sweat, but I'll stick to
my threadbare pajama tees put back on
after a shower, tucked up under these DDDs.

I keep the furnace at 68 degrees.
I keep the a/c at 68 degrees.

You're always cold. I'm always hot.

& rarely dry.

One kid taught me what his father taught him:
*you don't need more than a handful.*

The magazine taught me self-exam: braless, put
a pencil under one, if it falls, you're perky.

Every time I write about sex it is a radical act because
sometimes I can't shake the early-formed urge
to cover my large breasts even though I've since
taught myself a deep V bestows a masterpiece
to anyone looking.

Blessed & divine accumulations of fat bouncing
in the rain-soaked run from lawn to parking lot.
We decided to leave before lightning shut down
Lilith Fair even though Jewel hadn't played
the main stage yet.

I was 19, my sister 16. Jewel was the only reason
those men were there. It wouldn't have been for
the Indigo Girls or Lisa Loeb.

*Holy Tits!* they yelled.

I wish I had found a safe place for us in the gap of
two front teeth, in between two guitars slung low,
in the curve of thick black spectacles.

I was angry at the feminist organizers too, shooting
off an email when I got home—*where are the f-ing
plus-size t-shirts?*

Every time I write about sex it is a radical act because five lbs. of fat are only holy with a nipple.

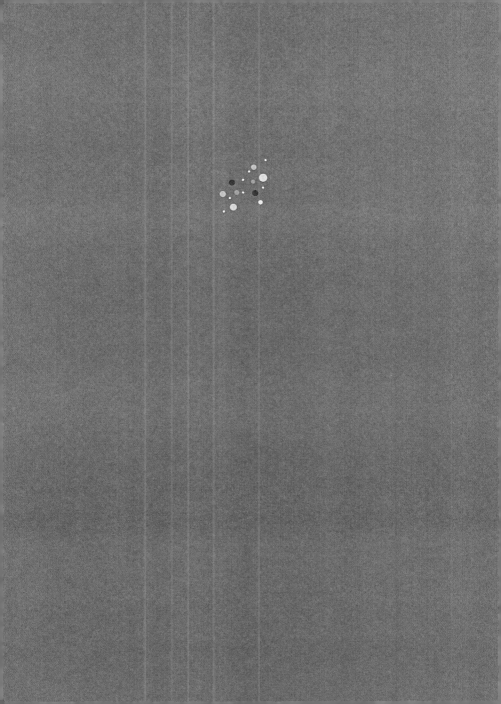

In the days of girls flipping up other girls' skirts
on the playground, upper elementary years,
I debated what part of my body I'd least want others
to see.

I decided if we ever switched to lifting each other's
shirts that would be the most embarrassing. Belly,
not boobs.

In the daze of my delayed girls-gone-wild phase,
late 20s/early 30s, my favorite bar Lou Magoo's
had buck-eighty-five PBR Light guzzlers & karaoke
Saturday nights.

The DJ's name was Sparkles. A friend made out
with a guy who said he was a jeweler, but neglected
to add *at Wal-Mart* until they were up against
a dumpster outside. Another friend always sang
"Back Door Man."

I showed my tits every week but never by lifting
my shirt, either by pulling it lower for maximum
cleavage or by popping one breast out—single
bull's-eye nipple in the smoky air.

do you remember the first time i took you to that bar
do you remember the shirt i wore the way the scoop
just grazed the top of my bra the chains attached at
each shoulder dangling deep do you remember the
way you looked at me do you remember that i had to
turn the lights off for months even after many nights
like that one drunk & groping

On those drunken nights, friends learned what
I sound like when we're having sex. First floor
bedroom with others sprawled on couches & living
room floor.

& because I want to live this love story as long
as I can, more people know now.

I'm taking the stairs at work, huffing after the first
flight.

If anyone is looking, they know what I look like
too. I've been to Yoga for Bigger Bodies.

Tucked my knees to my chest & breathed &
breathed & breathed.

I've been a Cat & a Cow.

I've put my ass in the air, face in the mat.

At the gym who I thought was the fattest woman
told me that I inspired her.

She kept coming because she knew she could do it
if I could do it.

Brave is exercising?
Brave is moving a fat body?

Guess I was the fattest woman to her.

*Brave* is existing.

Instagram post of fat woman in denim overalls
happy they came in her size, admitting she's just
now becoming comfortable with her #vbo.

Sometimes I have to google internet-speak.

Hey, I have that!

& I usually try to hide it.

Brave is a hashtag?

Brave is Visible Belly Outline?

Damn right it is. Every day it is.

i know you remember me flat on my stomach asking
without words for you to find that spot on my back
i know you remember how to tongue it how to taste
salt & smoke & everything about a saturday night
i know you remember me rarely rolling over without
my arms across my stomach my stomach hidden &
neglected & unloved even in the dark

Imagine ignoring erogenous zones because they are too big. *Too big.*

Really, imagine that.

A few months before we started dating I went into
a palm reader's tent in Atlantic City. I walked back
to the ocean sidestepping debris in the old sand.

I can't remember the feel of her hand on mine, or if
she traced her fingertip across my palm as she read.

She told me I would be changing jobs, would start
working with kids. I had just finished a teaching
degree & was about to start job searching. Damn.
She was good.

Then she said I would find love.

Fraud.

I was so alone.

A few months earlier than that, you were drunk
with your cousin & his girlfriend watching
the Black Eyed Peas on Dick Clark's Rockin' Eve.
You never introduced a girlfriend to the family.
They all thought things.

I heard the story of that night when I met your
family later that same year (guess the palm reader
was right...)

how you loudly told them you'd fuck Fergie

how you slid down the stairs on a collapsed
cardboard box

how you were accused of pissing on the dog's back
as you pissed off the back porch

Twelve years before Atlantic City, I asked the Ouija
Board if I already knew the person I'd marry.

The Ouija Board said YES, planchette swinging
towards J when I asked who.

We knew each other in high school, but lost touch
for fifteen years.

I was dating Jim. I hated him. I hated him
for a long time after.

Three years before Ouija at graduation ceremony
practice, I remember telling you my cap was too
tight—6 5/8 instead of the 7 5/8 they measured
around my fat head & curls.

I slapped at the Ouija Board & stood up.

My gown didn't fit either. I cut long slits under
the arms so it wouldn't be as tight across my chest.

When I picked up the heart-shaped planchette,
the plastic bubble had cracked.

You have always been M: *Mike. Mine* even if
I didn't know it.

J and M are at the same corner of the board.

Now I look at my palm: heart lines long & curved
like the heavy pull of breasts but only visible when
I start to close my fat fists, flesh folding on itself,
revealing.

i have never known a body that didn't touch itself
half moons of darkened skin under breasts
b-belly double bumps that shift & wiggle with
the slightest brush

we know hands strong enough to lift

fingers nimble enough to open flesh whether thighs
or lips

& when we kiss—

when you kiss my neck i am every cliché i am meant
to be denied

      jelly

                   aflutter            stars

                       so bright

Fuck the friend flippant enough to say *by the way my marriage advice: don't.* I'm tired of benefits-of-the-doubt. That wasn't his messy divorce talking. *And if you do, be happy with whatever it is looking back at you across the table.* Am I too sensitive to assume a subtle eating metaphor only came out for his fat friend?

One of our best tables was a Christmas gift to each other. Nine course tasting menu at the chef's table tucked into the busy kitchen corner.

Single spoon of foie gras mousse & two cranberry slices bright. Sashimi with spicy soy & kumquat. Chestnut agnolloti, golden pickled beets, lamb three ways. Chocolate ganache, pistachio tuile.

We sat beside each other watching the sous chefs, the bustle & bread delivery basket back & back & back for more, steam & heat & sweat. Am I employing a metaphor?

I'm happy with whatever it is we see in front of us.

"The Power of Love" was on the retro radio station the first time we had sex. Every time I write about sex with you, I am also writing about love.

& every time I write about love it is so fucking radical.

I bought a t-shirt recently: *Thick Thighs Save Lives*. It's the truest piece of clothing I own.

you tell me i deserve this being in love this love this
happiness this happily ever after you tell me after
everything i deserve this you tell me i deserve to kiss
& be kissed to love & be loved to see & be seen you
tell me i deserve this i deserve this i deserve to be this
to be this happy

The Lindy West epigraph is from her memoir *Shrill: Notes from a Loud Woman* (Hatchette Books, 2016).

The board game True Colors (Pressman Toy Corporation) has included various subtitles on the different editions of its box, including "Do you see yourself as others see you?" and "What do your friends REALLY think of you?"

Fat Monica appeared in only four episodes of the 10-season run of *Friends*, but she was referenced in nearly half of the episodes.

The poem "I used too many calendars…" borrows from a stanza in Andrea Gibson's poem "Staircase" on the album *Flower Boy*: "I say, / 'In the ghost town of our love / There is a player piano / Trying to prove it can make music / Without being touched. / My fingertips / Miss her / So much.'"

A 2005 study "Obesity Stigma in Sexual Relationships" by Eunice Y. Chen and Molly Brown had participants rank their preference for dating persons who are healthy, who are missing their left arms, who use wheelchairs, who have histories of mental illness including suicide attempts and self-harm, who have a history of curable STIs, and who are obese.

In April 2013 Target apologized for a product-naming discrepancy in which the same dress was labeled "dark heather gray" for straight sizes, but "manatee gray" for plus sizes.

The closing credits of *Bridesmaids*, a 2011 comedy film, are played over an extra scene showing the actors Melissa McCarthy and real-life husband Ben Falcone engaging in sexual acts involving a foot-long sandwich.

The poem "A group of men were harassing me..." is dedicated to my sister Julia Jackson and my friend SuzAnne Sisak.

"Mama" Cass Elliott, the American singer and actress best known as a member of the group The Mamas & The Papas, died on July 29, 1974 when she was 33-years-old, approximately nine months after the *Scooby Doo, Where Are You?* episode with her guest appearance aired.

His name was CJ.

In *Shallow Hal*, a 2001 comedy film, Gwyneth Paltrow's fat suit only weighed twenty-five pounds, yet made her character Rosemary appear approximately 350 pounds, and it was rumored that Jack Black actually had to lose weight to play the title character.

The ending of the poem "One kid taught me what his father taught him..." echoes a Facebook status by poet Diamond Forde: "I'm a very charitable person. Every time I wear a low cut shirt I'm technically donating a work of art to the masses."

Lilith Fair was a woman-only music festival founded by Sarah McLachlan. It took place during the summers of 1997 to 1999 and was revived in 2010 with limited success. In 1997 Lilith Fair was the top-grossing touring festival and the 16th highest grossing among all concert tours.

The poem "In the daze of my delayed girls-gone-wild phase…" is dedicated to Julia, Scoots, Drewby, Colby, BJ and Kimberly (who shouldn't have been so scared), Lil Rob, Sheila and Frankie Baby, Junior, Goober, The Drape, Lou, and Sparkles herself.

I am so grateful for poet and fat-activist Rachel Wiley—for her #vbo and for her poem "belly kisses" included in her collection *Nothing is Okay* (Button Poetry, 2018).

The 1985 single "The Power of Love" by Huey Lewis and the News was written by Huey Lewis, Chris Hayes, and John Colla for the *Back to the Future* movie soundtrack and includes the lyric "…*[love] might just save your life.*"

ACKNOWLEDGMENTS

Grateful acknowledgment is made to the editors of the following journals in which excerpts originally appeared: *The Boiler*, *Construction*, *Puerto del Sol*, *Rabbit Catastrophe Review*, *Rogue Agent*, *SWWIM Every Day*, *The Voices Project*, and *Uppagus*.

The poem "there was a kiss electric..." was included in FREE FUCKING POEMS FOR FREE, a mini-book published by Hyacinth Girl Press.

*

Thank you to my best readers: Lisa Alexander, Tess Barry, Rachel Mennies, Emily Mohn-Slate, Michelle Stoner, and Bernadette Ulsamer.

Thank you, Jan Beatty, for creating the space where all the best readers and writers flourish.

Thank you, Kayla Sargeson, for being the poet-crush who never fades.

Thank you, Elizabeth J. Colen, for being the very first reader of this piece when it was only a dozen pages long. You gave me the confidence to continue writing.

Thank you to these writers for sharing important conversations with me as this book came to be: Jessica Rae Bergamino, Kayleb Rae Candrilli, Anne Champion, Diamond Forde, James Allen Hall, Daniel M. Shapiro, and Rachel Wiley.

Big, fat thanks to everyone at YesYes Books, especially KMA Sullivan for believing in this book.

Thank you, Mom, again for everything.

Thank you, Julia, for being my strong connection to the past, my eagle-eye for FP in the present, and who I'm sure will be my best friend always.

Thank you, Mike, for being supportive as I share the details of our marriage. The best of us isn't on these pages. The best of us is something we share only with each other. Thank you for always seeing me. I love you.

PHOTO BY MIKE BERRY

JENNIFER JACKSON BERRY is the author of *To Know Crush* (YesYes Books, 2020) and *The Feeder* (YesYes Books, 2016). Her chapbook *Bloodfish* was published in 2019 by Seven Kitchens Press as part of their Keystone Chapbook Series. She lives in Pittsburgh, Pennsylvania.

FICTION

*Girls Like Me* by Nina Packebush

RECENT FULL-LENGTH COLLECTIONS

*Ugly Music* by Diannely Antigua

*Gutter* by Lauren Brazeal

*What Runs Over* by Kayleb Rae Candrilli

*This, Sisyphus* by Brandon Courtney

*Salt Body Shimmer* by Aricka Foreman

*Forever War* by Kate Gaskin

*Ceremony of Sand* by Rodney Gomez

*Undoll* by Tanya Grae

*Everything Breaking / For Good* by Matt Hart

*Sons of Achilles* by Nabila Lovelace

*Landscape with Sex and Violence* by Lynn Melnick

*GOOD MORNING AMERICA I AM HUNGRY AND ON FIRE*

    by jamie mortara

*Stay* by Tanya Olson

*a falling knife has no handle* by Emily O'Neill

*One God at a Time* by Meghan Privitello

*I'm So Fine: A List of Famous Men & What I Had On* by Khadijah Queen

*If the Future Is a Fetish* by Sarah Sgro

*Gilt* by Raena Shirali

*Boat Burned* by Kelly Grace Thomas

RECENT CHAPBOOK COLLECTIONS

*Vinyl 45s*

    *Inside My Electric City* by Caylin Capra-Thomas

    *Exit Pastoral* by Aidan Forster

    *Of Darkness and Tumbling* by Mónica Gomery

    *The Porch (As Sanctuary)* by Jae Nichelle

    *Juned* by Jenn Marie Nunes

    *Unmonstrous* by John Allen Taylor

    *Preparing the Body* by Norma Liliana Valdez

    *Giantess* by Emily Vizzo

*Blue Note Editions*

    *Beastgirl & Other Origin Myths* by Elizabeth Acevedo

    *Kissing Caskets* by Mahogany L. Browne

    *One Above One Below: Positions & Lamentations* by Gala Mukomolova

*Companion Series*

    *Inadequate Grave* by Brandon Courtney

    *The Rest of the Body* by Jay Deshpande